Inclusive Leadership

Unleashing the Power of People

Mason Duchatschek
Dr. Amy Alfermann
Rev. Sheila Bouie-Sledge

Inclusive Leadership:
Unleashing the Power of People

Table of Contents

Chapter 1:
Missing the Cut

This book was written:

1. To identify and protect you against managerial blind spots you didn't know existed.

2. To help you understand your personal strengths and opportunities for improvement.

3. To help you recognize strengths and opportunities for improvement in others.

4. To help you learn to build teams of people with complementary skills, knowledge, abilities, perspectives, and interests.

5. To help you understand why it is important to embrace diverse perspectives when making decisions.

6. To help you understand how to turn adversaries into allies.

7. To help you eliminate interpersonal and organizational conflict so people and teams accomplish more, faster.

I grew up in a small community of about 10,000, in a middle-class suburb about 30 miles south of St. Louis. My mom taught 5th grade and my dad was in sales.

Summers were spent outside, playing whiffle ball or touch football in the yard with the other kids in the neighborhood, playing hockey in the street, or shooting hoops in the driveway. We walked or rode our bikes everywhere we went—without helmets, of course.

My parents had reasonable rules. Tell the truth. Let them know where we were, who we were with, and when we would be back, and call if there were changes to our plans. We also had to come home when the streetlights came on.

My parents never pushed anything on us. They always encouraged us to make our own decisions. They supported our decisions once we made them.

By contrast, Sheila grew up in a family that was more likely to help guide her decision making. If her parents suggested something, she usually agreed, and trusted more in their judgement than her own. For example, her parents wanted her to get involved in scouting because they felt it would expose her to a variety of people who wanted to learn new things, earn recognition, start and finish tasks, and have fun. Because they insisted, Sheila made new friends and discovered a different world outside of her neighborhood that she wouldn't have otherwise.

If, or should I say when, we showed an interest in playing competitive sports, my parents encouraged us and supported us. All they asked was that we did our best, demonstrated good sportsmanship, and didn't quit.

Beginning at age 7, and up until we were old enough to participate in middle school and high school athletics, my brother and I got to compete in YMCA basketball, floor hockey, baseball, junior league football, local swim meets, and AAU track and field.

In the team sports, the spotlight didn't usually shine on me or anything I did. Why? Because there were always other kids who were bigger, faster, or stronger or had more skills.

I don't remember being any game hero. But I don't remember ever screwing something up so bad that I was the goat either. I just remember doing my part and doing it in a fun way with friends.

Some of the teams won. Others lost. As a member of various teams, I got to experience what it was like to celebrate championships and accomplish goals. I also knew what it was like to be on a team that came up short and suffered disappointment. Our coaches always acknowledged our effort, told us what we needed to learn and work on, and encouraged us to try again next time, because back then there was always next year.

Knowing there was always another season, one more shot, seemed to take the sting of losing away. Sometimes it helped more than others, but it always made me feel better knowing we had another chance.

Junior high and high school can be awkward times for lots of people and for many different reasons. Some people get bad skin. Others get tall and awkward. Some struggle with weight. I had a different problem, and it involved height and weight, but not what some of you might expect.

I made the school basketball team in 8th grade and got cut in 9th. I felt sad, frustrated, left out, and all the other emotions that go along with that kind of public embarrassment and humiliation.

I'll never forget seeing the list of names on the locker room wall. The guys that made the list were jumping around high-fiving each other while I looked at the list again and again as if I might have overlooked the name Duchatschek on a list of 15 names. I looked around and saw three or four other people looking as dumbfounded, confused, embarrassed, humiliated, and stunned as I felt.

Speaking of what I felt, I remember this nauseous feeling, like a volcano ready to erupt in my stomach. I remember the lump in my throat, and I didn't say a word because I didn't want anyone to hear my voice crackle.

The coaches didn't want me on the 9th grade team. I missed the cut. It took everything I had to hold back the water that was swelling in my eyes. Everything.

After I had time to process what had happened, I knew what I needed to do. The answer was: the best I could with what I had. I had a decent cross country season and did make the varsity roster, so I decided to apply my efforts toward running during basketball season in the hopes that it would better prepare me for track season and, with a little luck, some more varsity action.

In hindsight, missing the cut for basketball shouldn't have been a surprise, because even though I hustled and tried really hard, the other kids really were more skilled. It probably didn't help that I was really short either. No matter how hard I tried, I wasn't tall enough and couldn't jump high enough to touch the net. Reasoning and logic didn't matter then. Not being on that team did. And it hurt.

With the exception of running, I can't say I was thrilled with the way high school was starting off, and things didn't really go up from there anytime soon after.

How small was I? When I got my driver's license at the beginning of 11th grade at 16, it said I was 5'2" and 95 pounds. I lied. I really weighed 88 pounds but figured I'd better add a few pounds for the lady at the Department of Motor Vehicles in case I grew.

I drove to restaurants and, more often than not, the servers brought me the kids' under-12 menu. When the movie *Ghostbusters* came out, my younger brother and his friends, who were three grades younger than me, offered to buy my ticket if I would drive them. All of us got in for under 12 except for one of my brother's friends.

Sheila teases me because she had the exact opposite experience. By her own admission, she was "tall, thin, and bony" and got hit with the adult fees for activities WAY before I ever did. She had bus drivers asking her what year she was born, because they were convinced she needed to pay adult fares. If she got out of line, adults treated her as if she was older than she was.

The kids I grew up playing sports with were now young men. I wasn't. Going through all of junior high and most of high school being stuck in the body of a 10-year-old made it very difficult to feel a part of the groups I had been a part of growing up.

While my friends were hoping for new cars, trucks, stereos, and speakers for their birthdays, I was praying for puberty. My prayers were finally answered my senior year.

When my voice changed and my body grew, I finally got to feel like part of the class again, for the first time in a long time—really since we were little kids. I got invited to parties. I was able to relate on a social and maturity level with kids my age, and with that came dates with some really great girls. And truth be told, that might have been my favorite part.

I learned valuable lessons. Moving forward, I made conscientious choices to include rather than exclude peers from activities. I looked for ways to make socially awkward circumstances less awkward for others whenever I noticed them. I've never forgotten how bad it felt to be an outsider and miss the cut, compared to what it felt like to be part of something and make a contribution.

Exercise #1:

Evaluate your life experiences and think of at least one thing (lesson, perspective, etc.) that stuck with you. What opportunity did it provide you to learn and develop character, personal strength, and/or awareness?

When it came time to look for a place to go to college, I discovered what I thought was a hidden gem about 125 miles from home. It was Westminster College, and it wasn't really hidden. It was in the town of Fulton, Missouri, a town of about 7,000 people, and had just under 1,000 students.

I say *hidden* because nobody from my high school went there. In fact, the only person I knew before I visited the campus was a friend of mine named Kris from a nearby high school with whom I occasionally ran during the summer. He was a year older than I was and made the college cross country team, and thought I could do the same given that I ran on our high school cross country team and we qualified for the state meet that year.

So, I went and checked it out. Their academic programs were excellent and exactly what I was looking for. The campus was beautiful. I felt comfortable. The library was quiet. The fraternities down the street had their stereos thumping. About 85% of the student body was associated with fraternities and sororities, and the energy of this place was impossible to ignore.

More than anything, I saw an opportunity for a fresh start. Nobody there really knew me or knew of me as the kid who didn't look old enough to drive, except for one person, and he didn't even go to high school with me.

As a bonus, William Woods was an all-girls college at the time, and it was just a mile down the road. The girl-to-guy ratio was something like 3 to 1 in the town of Fulton, and the more I heard about this place, the more I liked it.

Because it was a private school, it cost about twice what it would have cost to attend the University of Missouri or any of the other state schools. The academic and athletic scholarships I was offered would help defray costs, and my parents were willing to make sacrifices and cover the difference if I wanted to go for it.

Shortly after being accepted, I got a call from an upper classman named Ivan. Ivan was the rush chairman and the one person in charge of recruitment for Phi Delta Theta, which was one of the seven fraternities on campus. He was also on the college cross country team and got my name off the list of incoming freshman.

Ivan called and invited me to what they called a pre-rush weekend at the end of the school year to further check out the college and fraternities—in particular, his. He mailed me a schedule of the weekend and it looked awesome.

The plan was for me to drive up there after school and spend Friday and Saturday night at the frat house and participate in their activities all weekend long and meet the guys. They had a BBQ Friday afternoon and the most amazing party I'd ever seen on Friday night. There were kegs flowing. The dance floor was jammed with hundreds of beautiful college women dancing and jumping around with the guys. A live band had the walls shaking, and it was long after 3 a.m. when I finally tired out. It was like I'd seen in the movies, except that it was really happening and I got to be part of it.

They had fun stuff planned all day Saturday, followed by another amazing party that night. And when I finally packed up my stuff and headed home on Sunday, I couldn't wait to come back. Ivan was great, and so were all the guys I met. I felt like I'd made 60 new friends.

It's been many years since then, and I remember that weekend like it was yesterday. I can still remember the name of the band: Network. There it was, written on the bass drum. It's a memory I won't ever forget.

Ivan gave me his home phone number and told me to call him during the summer when it came time to fill out my class preferences for the college. When I got the stuff from the college, I called him. He invited me over to his parents' house, which was only an hour or so away, and he helped me create a schedule of ideal classes and professors so my college experience would begin on a good note.

When my friend Kris, who was in a different fraternity, called later in the summer, he was willing to help me pick out classes too. I thanked him but told him about my weekend visit with the Phi Delts, and that they had already helped me. He kept kind of quiet, and I didn't get to see him until school started.

When I got to campus, I found out there were strict rules that prohibited members of all fraternities from talking to freshmen until after the recruitment week, known as formal rush, was over.

Here's how the formal rush process worked. All the freshmen that wanted to join a fraternity were put into groups of around 25 or 30 people, and each group was taken to each of the seven fraternities for a meet-and-greet-type party that lasted about an hour. In that hour the fraternity members talked about their academic, athletic, intramural, and philanthropic achievements and why freshmen should want to join their fraternity. They also set aside time for conversations with freshmen to evaluate them as potential members. The first round of parties was a chance for freshmen and upperclassmen to feel each other out.

After the first round, the freshmen picked the three fraternities they were most interested in taking a second look at. In the second round of parties, the freshmen got to spend another hour at each fraternity they had listed as their top three choices.

Upperclassmen further evaluated the freshmen. The freshmen further evaluated their choices.

On bid night, each fraternity had a limit of 20 bid cards they could offer to freshmen according to college rules. They rank-ordered the freshmen that were interested in joining their fraternity, much like pro sports teams do when they draft players from college. They think about things like chemistry and how a person will contribute to their organization.

In the last round of parties I selected Ivan and Kris's fraternities and one other that I never seriously considered.

Because Ivan and Kris both ran cross country, Ivan knew that Kris was a friend from home. I liked and respected Ivan enough to be honest. I told him that I loved the guys at the Phi Delt house, but I was torn because I was also friends with Kris and felt his fraternity was full of nice guys too.

I told Kris the same thing. I didn't want either Kris or Ivan to feel like I didn't appreciate them or their fraternity. I didn't want either to feel that I betrayed them, especially if they campaigned on my behalf to get me a bid.

On bid night, an upper-class member of each fraternity was supposed to lead a group of freshmen down to their house to receive their bids and kick off a bid day party.

I saw the group of guys going to Kris's fraternity. I saw Ivan and the group of guys assembling to go to the Phi Delt house.

I felt conflicted. I felt pressure. I felt I had made new friends at the Phi Delt house that I didn't want to betray. They were so nice, genuine, helpful, and fun that I would have felt like a total traitor and scoundrel if I didn't pick them.

It was the moment of truth. At the last second I made my choice. I went up to Ivan and joined that group of guys. I remember going up to him moments before we were supposed to run down to the house and get our bids.

And then I just apologized for seeming so wishy-washy, thanked him for all he did to help me during the summer and all the great people he introduced me to, and told him that I was so excited to be going Phi Delt, and that after thinking about it, I knew in my gut it was the right choice. I couldn't have been happier.

I felt so relieved; the stress was gone. I made my decision. Time to run down to the house and start my first weekend at college with a bang!

The clock struck eight, and as soon as the church bells in the freshman quadrangle started ringing, each group of guys took off running toward the fraternity they were going to spend the next four years of their lives being part of.

Ivan led our group. When we got inside the house, there was a big foyer and a stairwell up to the second and third floors. Everybody was jumping around. Hugs, high-fives, handshakes.... Then a guy from the second floor called a freshman's name and he ran up the stairs, grabbed a bid card, and came running back down the stairs while everyone else cheered and yelled. Then another name got called, and another, and another, and another. They called the 20th name. It wasn't mine.

I had been in college one week. And not more than 10 minutes earlier, I was thinking that I couldn't ask for a better start with a great group of 60 new friends and how awesome it was going to be to be part of this group.

In the time it took to say one last name, that all changed.

Past that, I don't remember hearing another voice, a song, a sound. Again, it was as if the world stopped turning. I looked around and saw three or four other people looking as dumbfounded, confused, embarrassed, humiliated, and stunned as I felt.

Again, I remember this nauseous feeling, like a volcano ready to erupt in my stomach. I remember the lump in my throat, and I didn't say a word because I didn't want anyone to hear my voice crackle.

I looked around, feeling as if I was in the locker room after 9th grade basketball tryouts double checking to see if my name was on the list and realizing that it wasn't.

The Phi Delts didn't want me on their team. I missed the cut. I was going to be an outsider, again.

I knew the familiar feeling of trying to hold back the water that was swelling in my eyes. I knew what to do. I'd felt it before. I looked straight ahead and walked out that front door and back to my dorm room.

Later that same night, one of the resident advisors in my dorm, who also happened to be the guy whose room I crashed in the whole Phi Delt party weekend the previous spring, invited me into his room and tried to explain what happened.

He told me that they weren't a bunch of backstabbers; they liked me and were sorry for the mix-up. They weren't sure I liked them enough and thought I was going to join my friend Kris's fraternity, so they gave my bid to another guy who they KNEW really wanted it. The bad news was that the rush recruitment rules dictated that since they had filled all of the 20 available positions, they couldn't offer me a bid until second semester, but they would if I wanted to wait.

Since I had to wait a semester, it gave me time to look at all of the fraternities for longer than a few hours before making a decision. I found the one that was best for me.

I was gun-shy and not so quick to forgive or trust. When it came to the Phi Delts, whether I did or didn't, I felt I had something to prove. I used that painful experience to excel, drive harder, and push farther out of my comfort zone when it came to academic, athletic, social, or leadership opportunities. Those experiences, as painful as they were, made me a better person and a more inclusive leader.

I was SO motivated to show those guys what they missed, I couldn't describe it to you. If you can't join 'em, beat 'em. That was my motto. I made the track team and the cross country team, and eventually walked on the college's junior varsity basketball team, which felt like a personal milestone, especially after being cut in 9th grade. It helped that I had finally grown to reach a height of 6 feet tall.

My motivation to excel was exponentially greater because I missed the cut. Regardless of whether I did or not, I FELT like I had something to prove and worked harder because of it. I became a more valuable team member to anyone who would have me. I took nothing for granted.

As a leader, if you stay on the lookout for others who might have "missed the cut" and/or got overlooked for whatever reason, then the simple act of reaching out to them and including them in your plans, when others choose not to, might likely contribute to a level of motivation, trust, and loyalty to your team that your rivals could only dream about.

Exercise #2:

Having a motto, life philosophy, or spiritual theme can be critical. Have you used one in the past? What is a challenge that you are currently facing? What motto have you been using to guide your response to the challenge?

Chapter 2:
Lead, Follow, or Get Washed Away

My junior year in college, I went outside of my comfort zone again. I applied for and earned an Army ROTC scholarship. The training was like a combination of playing a college sport, being part of a worthwhile organization, and taking college academic classes all in one. Little did I know then that a few years later, I wouldn't be "playing Army" to win any championship at the end of a season, but to help save a town from destruction during the Great Flood of 1993 in a small, historic Missouri town on the shores of the Mississippi River. If we failed, there wouldn't be any "next year" or "next season" to try again, or coaches to tell us we gave a good effort. It wasn't about making a team or winning trophies, titles, or bragging rights. It was about saving a town.

Of all the teams I've ever played on or groups I've been a part of, my unit in the 1140th Engineer Battalion of the Missouri Army National Guard was my favorite. I discovered personal strength in myself and in others. I saw perseverance, determination, and teamwork in people and places where the spotlights don't shine and that reporters don't write about. I saw real people overcome overwhelming odds and challenges using leadership, teamwork, and trust.

Six inches—that was all that stood between the top of levy I was standing on and the raging waters of the Mississippi River. That day, in the summer of 1993 in the historic town of Ste. Genevieve, Missouri, a little over an hour south of St. Louis, there was only 6 inches of clearance on the manmade levy protecting this small town of 3,000-4,000 people and the rich history that went with it.

The flood waters were rising an inch an hour. There I was with nearly 112 other soldiers representing Delta Company of the 1140th Engineer Battalion in the Missouri Army National Guard, and we all had one job. It was to save this town.

In order to do that, we would have to work hand in hand with civilian authorities and local volunteers to build a levy faster than the water was rising and build it well enough to withstand the continual barrage of water rushing against it nonstop until the river receded back into its banks. And none of us knew how long that would be. The first of many glaring problems was that I was a young and relatively inexperienced officer, a second lieutenant in charge of a platoon full of men, and I didn't know how to build a levy. I'm not convinced any of us did, but we were willing to learn. We had to, and fast.

Keep in mind that with the exception of one weekend a month, plus two weeks a year, I wasn't thinking about the Army at all. None of us were. We were civilians. We got up, worked out, came home, got showered, put on our work clothes, went to work, and came home. It was the usual stuff, day in and day out.

I woke up THAT day thinking like a civilian, but everything changed when I got "the call" later in the day activating our unit for State Emergency Duty. Just a few hours after getting "the call," I found myself standing on a levy looking down at the drops of sweat that were leaving spots in the dust covering my previously polished and spit-shined black leather boots. The brown t-shirt I wore under my pressed uniform was soaked. Some of the sweat was from the heat. The rest was from nerves.

I knew what was at stake. This wasn't an exercise or a drill. If we failed, good, kind people would lose their homes and everything in them, including irreplaceable pictures and family heirlooms.

The town was built by French colonists and was filled with historic homes, many dating back to late 1700s and early 1800s. It was, and still is, a community rich with history and tradition.

It was the kind of place where the neighbors knew each other by name. Children's bikes were parked on porches or left in their yards. Kids didn't feel a need to lock them up or chain them to immovable objects. It was filled with quaint restaurants, mom-and-pop shops full of crafts and antiques, bed-and-breakfasts, etc. It was just that kind of town.

Unfortunately, the original settlers built it REALLY close to the Mississippi River. The river had overflowed its banks, kept rising, and wasn't showing any signs of going anywhere but up anytime soon.

Adding to the pressure was the national media presence that had descended upon the area. CNN, CBS, ABC, you name it—the big network TV stations were all there!

The last thing I wanted was to be responsible for letting the community down. The second to last thing I wanted was to have the whole world know on national TV that something I did or didn't do caused an unnecessary breach in the levy and cost these people everything.

After all, upriver, levees were breaking and towns were being flooded. It was a regular occurrence. I'm sure the people in the media thought it was just a matter of time until the river got the best of this town too.

Fortunately, the people of Ste. Genevieve thought otherwise. So did our troops.

The mayor, Bill Anderson, was an older gentleman. He was a very nice man who was kind of tall, with gray hair and a calm, relaxed demeanor, like a grandpa. When we arrived in Ste. Genevieve, he had his leadership team and a plan of action already in place.

There were two streams running through the town toward the Mississippi River that divided the town into thirds. Responsibility for coordinating and managing local resources for each section of town—the north, central, and south—was assigned to a civilian authority.

Twenty years earlier, in 1973, there had been a flood that reached 43 feet above flood stage. It was the largest flood in recorded history in Ste. Genevieve until this one.

Fortunately, the mayor, along with the heads of the local emergency task force and levee districts, knew who had experience fighting the flood back then. The locals who were there during the flood of 1973 knew exactly where the flood waters would rise along the creek beds and along the Mississippi.

Captain Stephen Kohl was our company commander, and he assigned one platoon of about 30 to 35 soldiers to each section. The platoon leaders, of which I was one, worked in cooperation with the civilian authority in our section.

I was responsible for leading the soldiers on the north side of town, along with a man by the name of Louie Sexauer who was the civilian authority for our section. Louie had a short, stocky frame and thin white hair that was usually covered up with his green John Deere cap. He provided leadership to the local civilians on the north side. He was probably 72 or 73 years old but had the fire and intensity of an old-school football coach in his early 30s. Because Louie had seen the flood 20 years earlier, he told us what needed to be done, how it needed to be done, and when it needed to be done.

It was a good thing, too, since, as I said earlier, I didn't know squat about how to build a sandbag levee. As a general rule, when I don't know how to do something, I ask lots of questions and I listen closely to those who do.

By the time Louie got finished with me, I knew EXACTLY how much sand to put in a bag. Too much sand caused problems. Too little sand caused different problems. Believe it or not, there is a right way and a wrong way to fill sandbags.

Oh, and plastic sheeting—there's a special way to lay it out and build it into a levy, too, so that it minimizes the damage water can do to your levy and helps it last longer. Louie knew all the secrets. He shared them with me, and I passed them on to the troops and civilian volunteers who came to pitch in.

After assembling his leadership teams and assigning areas of responsibility, the mayor went to work assigning responsibility and accountability for the support functions, as well. He had people that were in charge of supplies like food, clean water, and first aid. He had people in charge of media relations, people in charge of quality control, to make sure that the levees were built correctly—the works.

Chapter 3:
Grace Under Pressure

When the first night came, it was just a race to see if we could raise the levees faster than the water was rising. Nobody got more than three hours of sleep that night—or the first three nights, for that matter. Lots of us didn't get any sleep. Somehow, we managed to fill sandbags and place them on the levee fast enough to keep the river from flowing over the top.

I really admired the leadership I saw that first night, and in the nights that followed too. No matter how scared, worried, or frantic the leaders around me felt, they never let it show. I did my best not to let my nerves show either. But it wasn't easy, at least for me.

My college ROTC instructor, Major Bill West, warned me and the other cadets about this very thing while we were going through our officer training. He told us in no uncertain terms that if we freaked out under pressure, so would the people we were supposed to be leading. If we could remain calm, then it was much more likely that our troops would remain calm too.

I kept his wisdom in mind and thought about my word choices and actions carefully. I got to see, hear, and feel the magic of his advice, live and in the flesh.

I'm not saying the leaders I answered to were pie-in-the-sky or "everything is going to be all right"-type cheerleaders. NO, it wasn't like that at all. It wasn't fake. They didn't sugarcoat our challenges. They kept things real, but never overreacted or rushed to any judgements.

Working with leaders like that made me feel better about what we were doing and our likelihood of success. I only hope that my efforts to do the same made the guys I was leading feel that way too.

I felt calm because the leaders I worked for, i.e., the mayor and my company commander, stayed calm. I felt confident because they showed confidence. I saw the importance of being calm and graceful under pressure firsthand, and it was a leadership lesson I will never forget.

Strategy Before Tactics

When the first long night ended and the first morning arrived on the north side of town where my unit was working, I noticed a couple of problems. The first problem was that there were sand piles dumped in the street every two to three blocks.

Prior to our arrival, the city had dumped piles of sand in what seemed like random places throughout the neighborhoods in the north side. Neighbors had been making sandbags on their own and hauling them with wheelbarrows and trucks to their homes, where many had started building their own sandbag levees to protect their individual homes.

Not only were the piles spread out, but some were placed in the low-lying areas near the main levee. So if a spot on the levee gave way or the river overflowed, it was highly likely that water could come rushing into where people were trying to work.

The second problem was a big one too. Because the sand piles were in random locations, lines of sight were nonexistent, and there was no good system in place by which people at one pile or place on a levee could communicate a problem to others in different places if something came up.

That morning, my platoon sergeant and I did some looking around...a little reconnaissance, if you will, with one purpose in mind. That purpose was to find an area close by that would solve both problems. We needed a high-ground place where everyone working would be safe, where we could communicate with everyone at once and see whatever resources were available or lacking at any given time.

The location we found to centralize and stage our north side operations was at the top of a hill next to a VFW hall that overlooked the river. It had a big, fully paved parking lot. On the other side of the road, across from the VFW hall, was an extra overflow gravel parking lot ,which gave us additional room to work.

The VFW hall was three blocks from the nearest point on the levee, and maybe eight to ten blocks from the furthest point. The road that ran between the paved VFW parking lot and the gravel overflow parking lot across the street ran right into the middle of the main levee section we were responsible for building and maintaining.

We found high, safe ground that wouldn't put people's lives at risk if the water got over or through the levee. There was room to load sandbags onto trucks. There was room and a reasonable surface to operate forklifts and lift pallets of sandbags into trucks. There were streetlights to make working at night easier and safer. And there were restrooms at the VFW, as well as a dining hall to accommodate the Red Cross and civilian volunteers.

For our intents and purposes, the VFW facility and the surrounding area was the most perfect and safe area we could find to stage our operations. From that moment on, all deliveries of raw materials or supplies were dropped off at the VFW instead of in random piles throughout the north side neighborhoods.

Just like the example the mayor gave when he divided the town into thirds, we divided our north side section of the main levee into thirds. We assigned responsibility for each third of our levee to a squad leader and his men.

Once the sandbags were filled, they were placed on wood pallets that were then loaded into the bed of our 5-ton army truck. Then the big truck full of sandbags would be directed to one of the three squad leaders closer to the front lines who needed it most, and the squad leader would direct the driver toward the place nearest the levee where the bags were needed. The guys would then carry and place the bags on the levee under the direction of their squad leader.

Because my squad leaders didn't have radios until after the second day, the truck drivers became our initial communication network. They were instructed to bring a report back to the staging area each time a driver came back, delivering messages from the squad leaders and informing me and my platoon sergeant of their worst-case scenario.

For example, one squad leader might send back a report indicating that there was a spot with 18 inches of clearance between the top of the levee and the river for a span of 200 meters. A second squad leader might indicate a span of 200 meters where there was only 6 inches clearance. And the third squad leader might report that his worst-case scenario at the time was 9 inches of clearance for 200 meters.

From a centralized staging area, given timely and accurate reports from squad leaders on the levee, a truck full of sandbags could be directed to the area of greatest need at any given time. The other platoon leaders like me who were responsible for saving other areas of the town did the similar things. They set up staging areas, as well, that looked a lot like ours.

When I tell the story that way, with the benefit of hindsight, it seems pretty uneventful, because those actions and choices just seem like common sense, don't they?

Well, they weren't, and here's why.

Sergeant Gary Wright was my platoon sergeant, and in a nutshell, he was a no-nonsense hardass. That's just one of the many reasons why I liked and respected him.

As a civilian, he was a supervisor who worked the production lines at an automotive assembly plant, and he didn't take crap from anyone.

In the five years that Sergeant Wright and I worked together, we only had two disagreements where I pulled rank on him and insisted that things be done my way instead of his. He was a smart and experienced soldier, and I respected him very much and listened carefully to his ideas.

I often asked for his perspective, and ended up doing things his way lots of times. Twice we disagreed and he ended up doing things my way.

The first time I pulled rank was when one of our guys got a bulldozer stuck in a creek in the jungle of Panama two years earlier. Sergeant Wright was pleasantly surprised when I figured out a way to get it unstuck that was different from his plan. The first morning of emergency flood duty was the second time.

Keep in mind that the floodwaters were rising an inch per hour, and from the moment we arrived, it took almost everything we had to get sandbags on the levee fast enough to stay ahead of the rising waters. When we arrived in Ste. Genevieve, it was an all-hands-on-deck-type thing and everyone was making, carrying, and throwing as many sandbags as they possibly could.

Sergeant Wright didn't think we had time to recon or figure out a plan for a staging area yet. He felt that having every person we could possibly have working at a sand pile was a necessity. He was focused on how many sandbags could be filled correctly and put onto the levee the right way.

Simply put, at a tactical level, he was focused on doing things the right way. At a strategic level, I was more concerned about keeping people safe and improving efficiency so we could get more accomplished faster. I felt it was more important to focus first on doing the right things, strategically speaking, before worrying about how to do things right, tactically speaking.

Privately, away from the guys, he made the case to me that we lacked the time to stop sandbagging and didn't have any spare time to find a staging area and/or move the guys up there.

I disagreed. However, I didn't blame him. I felt his sense of urgency. I shared his sense of responsibility, and then I took it from him. I told him I would accept 100% of the blame if I was wrong.

I didn't have the luxury of thinking all this through at the time. But as I look back, I was thankful that he was focused on doing things the right way. I'm thankful he felt comfortable voicing his disagreements with me. I'm thankful that he fully supported my decision after I made it, even though he disagreed with it. I'm also thankful that my instincts that day had me focused more on what I felt was important than on what I felt was urgent, and that I felt comfortable accepting responsibility for the outcomes of my decisions, as risky as they seemed then.

I can still remember him scrunching up his face and shaking his head at me. "OK, sir," he said. Then he went to work as if it was his idea and he supported it all along.

But why? I have a theory.

There are very few things I like less than being given responsibility for specific results and then having little to no authority over how those results would be accomplished. I certainly wasn't going to do that to him, and I didn't. He rewarded me by working his tail off to support me and got the rest of the guys to do the same.

Chapter 4:
Shared Responsibility and Engagement

Not quite 24 hours after we arrived, in the afternoon of our first full day of duty and in spite of our best efforts, things didn't look good on the north side. And, frankly, a few people in town were starting to whisper and wonder if the north side wasn't already a lost cause.

Louie and I got word that we needed to go to the mayor's office for a meeting. When we got there, it was me, Louie, my company commander, the mayor, and a few of the mayor's top advisors.

The mayor calmly looked at us and said, "I'm thinking we should transition from a levee-building operation into an evacuation mission on the north side."

If he followed through, it would create a dilemma.

Politically speaking, how could he just arbitrarily choose which part of town would get resources that could save it, while another part was evacuated, and was likely to get washed away? After all, he was elected to serve ALL the people in his community, not just those with the most valuable properties and businesses.

You could see the wrinkles on his forehead get deeper as he struggled with idea of making a decision that might make him appear to be playing favorites. What he did next was brilliant.

In the face of all that pressure, he asked for input, evaluated the ideas, and made a quick decision. One of the advisors raised his hand and said, "You shouldn't HAVE to make that decision. Why don't you let the community decide for themselves? If they want to save the north side, give THEM the chance to do it. Tell them that if we don't have 150 volunteers at the VFW on the north side tonight at 6 p.m., then we will go into evacuation mode. If this community wants to save the north side, then it is up to them, their families, and their friends to show up, step up, and save it."

The mayor did exactly that. He put out the word to the local media that if there weren't 150 volunteers present at the VFW at 6 p.m. that night, they wouldn't be able to hold and would begin evacuations.

The mayor told the truth. He didn't paint a picture worse than he saw it, or better than he saw it. He told it like it was and asked for help by including others in the problems-solving process. His message was simple and straightforward: "If you want to save the north side, you need to show up, and you need to step up."

You know what happened? He got his 150 volunteers and then some.

We lined up up in a big line and had them count off—1, 2, 3, 1, 2, 3, 1, 2, 3—until everybody had a number.

The 1s formed one group and were handed shovels. The 2s formed another group and were given sandbags and taught how to properly fill and tie them. The 3s formed a final group, and they carried the sandbags to the pallets so they could be loaded on the trucks and sent down to the people offloading them on the levee.

There were young kids, young adults, and grandparents there. You name it. They all showed up and contributed to the effort.

The leadership lesson I saw played out before my eyes that day was to find ways to make decisions WITH people, not FOR them.

Focus on Solutions

In the book of Matthew, Chapter 7, Verse 7, of the The Bible, it says that if you ask, you shall receive. There was something I noticed early on, and it continued throughout the time I was there. The community leaders in Ste. Genevieve made a habit of asking "how" questions rather than "why" questions.

Let me explain. I didn't hear any wimpy whining or questions like "Why is this happening to us?" or "Why can't this just be over?" Rather, I heard a lot of "how" questions, like "How can we do this better?" or "How can we do that faster?" Well, they asked everybody, and the answers started coming.

The Mississippi Lime Company is one of the largest employers in the county, and they came up with the idea of working on a holiday schedule to free up people from work so they could come help as volunteers with the sandbagging.

At one point, a little boy along with his grandfather came up to me and said, "Mister, we made this little chute in our wood shop downstairs." Then they showed me a little invention they made with what used to be a sheet metal vent that was cut in half. It was wide at the top and narrow at the bottom, and it angled downward on four wooden legs.

Their idea was that it would be easier and faster for people with shovels to put the sand in the wide end of the chute and let it slide down into a sandbag than it would be to try to get it in a bag every time using a shovel. They were right. It was faster and easier, and far less sand got spilled.

I called City Hall and told them about this little contraption, and less than an hour later, a carpenter came by, took his little notepad, scratched out a few designs, and said, "How many do you want, Lieutenant?"

In what seemed like no time at all, we had 20 of those things at my worksite alone. The other staging areas got some too.

After seeing how well those worked, someone else thought of taking a cement truck, attaching a conelike device at the end of the chute, and using it to fill bags with sand just like the people at Dairy Queen fill soft-serve ice cream cones from the machine.

Local power sports stores lent us ATVs, little four-wheelers, and three-wheelers so we could get up and around the levees faster.

A nearby penitentiary sent work crews of inmates who were short on time and had demonstrated good behavior who were also willing to pitch in and work hard. Every person who made and put sandbags on the levee made a difference.

So, the way I figure it is this. If you ask and you're going to receive, you might as well ask "how" questions focused on solutions instead of "why" questions focused on problems.

Chapter 5:
Adversity as a Blessing and Thinking Ahead

One morning, we got a flat tire on our 5-ton army truck that we were using to haul sandbags from the VFW staging area to the levee. Bad news, right?

The water was still rising rapidly. The only truck we were using to get bags to the levee wasn't working. And we had just found out it was going to be an hour or more until the truck was going to be fixed.

Have you ever had that sinking feeling in your stomach? You know the type. Well, that morning, it was alive and well inside of me. Rather than asking "why" questions, we started asking "how" questions, like how ELSE could we do this?

The answer we came up with was using pickup trucks. It should have been obvious, but until that moment, when we needed it the most, it wasn't.

Prior to that flat tire on our 5-ton Army truck, it never crossed our minds to use civilian pickups. The flat tire wasn't an obstacle. It was a blessing.

Within minutes, the mayor had the local media calling for volunteers who could drive pickups and deliver sandbags to the levee. The pickups were way more effective than our big 5-ton Army truck, because they could get closer to the levee, and that meant it took less manpower to put bags where they needed to go.

The pickup trucks could also go into tight places where the bigger truck wouldn't have gone. Wait times for squad leaders to get bags were drastically reduced, and we had more drivers able to get more bags to the levees faster.

I remember a gray-haired fellow, probably 55 or 60 years old, who came up to me, gave me the keys to his truck, and said, "Son, I have to work today and I can't help, but I'd like to, so here are the keys to my truck. I heard you guys needed pickups, and I heard you needed drivers. It's full of gas, and it is ready go. When you guys are done, all I ask is, just leave it at City Hall with the keys in it, and just leave me enough gas to get to the station, and I hope it helps."

Sure, it would have been easy to get down and frustrated when our vehicle became inoperable, but we didn't. **Instead, we made a conscious choice to look for opportunities in obstacles.**

Exercise #3:

Consider some of your previous personal and/or professional obstacles. What opportunities or advantages did they give you? What potential opportunities or advantages can you take away from current obstacles or challenges?

Thinking Ahead

After about three days and nights, our soldiers were past the point of being productive because of the lack of sleep and intense physical and emotional demands being placed upon them. Our commander required that each platoon divide into a night shift and a day shift, with each 12 hours long so we could have 24-hour coverage on the levees without becoming wandering, aimless zombies.

I took half of my platoon, and we worked from 6:00 in the morning until 6:00 in the evening. Sergeant Wright, my platoon sergeant, took the other half of the unit from 6 p.m. until 6 a.m. In the middle of the night, Sergeant Wright knew he wouldn't have but a fraction of the civilian volunteers working with his guys that I had working with mine.

In the daytime, there were actually several windows of opportunity where we could make more sandbags than we could distribute. So he pulled me aside and pointed over to a vacant portion of the parking lot. "See that space? It should be full of pallets loaded with sandbags. We should probably have a few trucks parked full of sandbags, too. Heaven forbid we got a soft spot in the levee and lost it all because we didn't have a contingency plan. If we got trucks and sandbags ready to go plug a leak, people in the staging area could jump in back and we could plug it fast with a massive wave of sandbags." **He knew as a leader that it was our responsibility to expect the best, but also to prepare for the worst.**

The "Least Bad" Choice

Not more than a couple of days later, his wisdom paid off. You see, the good people of Ste. Genevieve are churchgoers—in fact, so much so that when Sunday morning came, we only had but a handful of volunteers sandbagging in our staging area. The vast majority of "regular" volunteers were in church.

There were two to three spots along our north side levee that needed attention, and there was minimal clearance above the river. By "minimal," I'm talking about a few inches.

We did the best we could with the soldiers and limited volunteers we had. My gut told me we could be in big trouble if that was going to be all the help we were going to get until noon when church got out.

I admit I was tired and edgy and was making a conscious effort NOT to overreact or panic, even though I felt like overreacting and panicking. I called my company commander and told him about the problems that were now weighing heavy on my mind..I asked for his help and guidance.

After working all night, Sergeant Wright and his guys had just eaten, showered, and fallen asleep on their cots that were spread throughout the basketball court in the high school gymnasium. A decision to wake them all up and have them put on their uniforms and come back out to help crossed my mind. It was a horrible thought. But I was afraid it was the right one.

The last thing I wanted to see happen was the levee on the north side failing. Deep down, I was betting that the guys felt the same way. At least I hoped so.

That was the decision I made, and calling it unpopular would be an understatement. I knew some of the guys would be cussing me out behind my back. I saw their heads shake in frustration and disbelief as they arrived on the work site. And I didn't blame them a bit.

We depleted the sandbags in the reserve stockpiles and got the bags to levee as fast as we could. Then we got the guys back to bed as soon as the volunteers started to show up again.

I felt I had two bad choices. The first risked losing the levee. The second risked angering the guys I depended on to get our work accomplished. When given the choice among several undesirable options, I knew I had to pick the "least bad" choice and drive on.

What was it that allowed me to make amends with the guys? Truth, humility, and honesty. I took the time afterward to explain what was going on and why I viewed waking them up as the "least bad" choice. I included them by sharing my experience and dilemma. They understood and all was forgiven.

I was amazed at what a little humility and honesty did to improve low morale. **As I reflect back on that incident all these years later, I'm reminded how important it is to explain the "why behind the what" when you ask people to do something, especially**

if it involves a change or decision that is certain to be unpopular.

Followership

The skill, initiative, and knowledge needed to envision and set up the staging area were not the same as what it took to KEEP things running well once it was set up. Once everyone understood their roles and duties, it almost ran itself.

Remember that story of Chicken Little? You know, "The sky is falling, the sky is falling!" I'm talking about that Chicken Little.

Well, I met my share of "Chicken Littles" in that situation. Just like I knew the sun would rise in the east and set in the west, on any given day at least two or three different well-intentioned people would come running up to me screaming "Emergency, emergency!" and try to tell me the levee was just about to break or get overrun.

I had squads and their leaders constantly monitoring their portions of the levee. If something was wrong, they knew it, and I got the message immediately by radio.

Access to my superiors, i.e., the big brass, who were operating out of the headquarters at City Hall, was easy at first. There was a bridge that crossed the creek separating the north and central sections of town, and it only took about 5 minutes to get there from the VFW.

It got more complicated and difficult when the floodwaters went over the top of the creek's bridge, and the fastest way to City Hall using rural secondary roads then became 25 minutes or longer one way.

In my absence, I needed someone that I could trust to run the staging area operation as it was supposed to be run. I didn't want anyone "reinventing" the systems I put in place.

I had U.S. Congressmen visiting my staging area along with full-blown colonels. The governor of Missouri even came by and visited with me. When I was gone, I didn't want anyone messing with my systems. To be more specific, I didn't need a LEADER. I needed an outstanding FOLLOWER.

Why? Had I left my post to the highest-ranking soldier under me, which in a textbook scenario I absolutely should have, then I would have risked them being tempted, despite the best of intentions, to make different decisions about how to run things **without the benefit of the information Sergeant Wright and I had when we set the systems up**.

Besides, they were doing the jobs that they had very well. My decision later generated a ton of controversy. But the textbook solution of leaving the job with the next-highest-ranking soldier would have been a mistake, and I knew it.

Instead, I sought out a soldier who was fresh out of basic training and was brand-new to our unit. I put him in charge of the staging area and explained **in detail** exactly what needed to be done and how.

Some of you might be thinking, *Mason, are you nuts? An 18-year-old private with no leadership experience? What the heck were you thinking?* My company commander always gave me space and usually let me call my own shots, but this idea even raised his eyebrows.

I wanted to leave things with the best follower, someone with incredible attention to the smallest details. Considering that my choices were other soldiers who were civilians 28 days of each month or someone who had just gotten out of basic training, I went with the new guy out of basic.

If you haven't been to basic training, let me give you a quick summary. It's a different world. The drill sergeants run it.

I went to basic in Fort Knox, Kentucky. On the bus ride from the airport to the post I met my first drill sergeant, and he looked at us and asked a few questions I never forgot. "How many of you are in Bravo Company?" A bunch of us raised our hands. "You're going to get tired of seeing me. How many of you are in 2nd Platoon of Bravo Company?" A group of us on the bus raised our hands. "You're going to get REAL tired of seeing me." He was right.

I hated basic training. I made the mistake of thinking it would be easy because I was in shape, loved getting up early, and didn't care if people yelled at me. I liked to think I was pretty smart, too, and that was my biggest problem.

For a few days, anyway, I thought I could find shortcuts or better ways of doing things. I was wrong and found myself doing pushups, lots of pushups—lots and lots of pushups—every time I failed to do exactly what I was told, exactly how I was told to do it, and exactly when I was told to do it.

It took me a few days before I realized that it was easier to tuck my bootlaces in my boots than do pushups. It was easier to make sure that there were no strings hanging from my uniform and that all my buttons were buttoned than it was to do pushups. I realized it was easier to keep my mouth shut and eat my food in the mess hall without saying a word or looking up than it was to have my food taken away and go the next few hours hungry. I learned it was easier to stand motionless in formation with my eyes looking directly in front of me than it was to do pushups. I realized it was easier to make sure my footlocker was locked than it was to go outside and pick up all the items that the drill sergeant had thrown out the window and put them back in my locker.

Drill Sergeant Michael Sabroe and Drill Sergeant Gregory Norfus were polar opposites, but both were very intense, and each of them had an attention to detail that was MICROSCOPIC.

One (Drill Sergeant Sabroe) was always yelling. The other (Drill Sergeant Norfus) had more of a silent intensity. I'm not convinced that Drill Sergeant Sabroe wasn't one of the last of the old-school soldiers who were given the choice of joining the Army or going to jail.

Their standards were clear and high. Before I was able to turn in my M16, I spent no less than 14 hours cleaning it with Q-tips, brushes, and pipe cleaners before Drill Sergeant Norfus allowed it to pass his inspection.

When I finished basic, I finally understood why there was so much importance placed on attention to detail. If each soldier isn't trained to pay strict attention to detail, they put the entire unit at risk.

Just imagine walking through the woods on a night patrol mission in enemy territory, worrying about whether or not someone forgot to push the safety button on their weapon. All it would take would be for one person to hit a branch or trip and fall and their weapon could go off and give away the position of the unit or actually shoot another member of the squad with not-so-friendly fire.

Let's go back to the flood. The rest of soldiers in my unit had been out of basic for a long time, and Private Cluck was fresh out; I knew his ability to follow **specific** directions **exactly** as they were told to him would be unmatched.

I felt in my gut that his sensitivity to detail and clear awareness of consequences if he failed would make him the perfect person to execute the operation I was going to give him.

He was the best follower in my unit. I told him how to do things once and I didn't have to repeat myself. I gave him a radio so he could call me if he had questions.

Sure enough, he delivered, and did so with flying colors. Just like I depended on private Cluck, my company commander depended on me to follow his specific instructions when they were given.

I had faith that my company commander had access to more and better information sources than I did when he made his decisions. Like the private, I could always ask questions or contribute new information for his consideration, but for whole thing to work and for us to win, there were numerous times when it was just as important, if not more important, for those of us with leadership roles to be good followers, not just guys barking orders.

I really got to see, hear, and feel how good followership was a key component of effective leadership.

Exercise #4:

Consider the people who depend on you and your abilities. In what ways can you become a better follower?

Chapter 6:
Good Decisions, Lower Risks, High Standards, and Sincere Appreciation

Better Decisions, Faster

When you're the leader, you're the judge. Not only do you need to determine how much information you need to feel certain about taking specific action, but you must have the ability to weigh the relative importance and accuracy of the information you have as well.

I own a business, and as I often do, I came home one day and asked my wife what her thoughts were on the challenge I was facing. She's smart and reasonable and has good judgment, so I value her opinion. Much to my surprise, she huffed, shrugged her shoulders, and gave me "the look"—you know the type. *Why should I bother answering your question, since you are just going to do what you are going to do anyway? You hardly ever listen to me.*

From her perspective, I could understand why she felt that way. After all, whenever I asked for her opinion, I frequently gave her the information pertaining to a small portion, or a single aspect, of the overall problem I was struggling with. And typically when I did so, it wasn't because I wasn't willing to share more information; it was because I didn't have the time. To her it seemed like I had plenty of time and was sharing all the information about my entire problem, when, in fact, I was just sharing a small portion of a much larger and more complex challenge.

On one particular day, I invested the time necessary to explain that I could be considering a half dozen or more factors or situations at any given time, and if she had access to all of the information and factors that I did when I made decisions, I felt she would make the same decisions I did, for the same or at least similar reasons.

So, it wasn't that I did not follow the advice I asked for. I just weighed it in comparison to many other, competing factors and elements. Then I made my decisions after considering many different perspectives of an overall picture.

As a general rule, "You hardly ever listen to me" is not something you want to hear from the variety of people you've chosen to surround yourself with. You never know what kind of groundbreaking ideas they may be willing and capable of sharing if you only ask and take the time to respectfully listen to what they have to say on a consistent basis. If you don't have enough time to explain the details involved in your most pressing decisions, I would at least encourage you to tell that to the people you depend on rather than letting them make other assumptions.

The mayor of Ste. Genevieve had assembled an all-star team of local leaders. Each of them was an expert in their field. He had knowledgeable and capable people who could help him make good decisions based on, not one perspective, but a 360-degree view of any situation. All of them knew he was pressed for time. Because the floodwaters continued to rise, he didn't have to explain anything in excessive detail to anyone to avoid hurt feelings or keep from risking a loss of engagement.

He had assembled people on this team who fought the largest flood that had ever been seen in his community. They knew where the water was going to come from and where it was going to go ahead of time. He had people who knew where and whom to call to get needed supplies. He knew where to get capable and willing heavy equipment and earthmoving equipment operators. He had people with local media contacts to get necessary information out quickly. He had technical experts who knew how to build and inspect levees. He had built an information gathering system that allowed him to gather a wide range of accurate facts and trustworthy opinions quickly. He included these people and their knowledge, experience, and perspectives in his decision-making processes.

Without trust, the mayor wouldn't have gotten the truth. Without the truth, he wouldn't have had the information he needed to make the best decisions.

The mayor did lots of things right, and he made good decisions quickly. I'm convinced that one of the most important things he did well was put himself in a position to make good decisions quickly, and that couldn't have happened if he **hadn't surrounded himself with such a wide variety and diverse range of outstanding people who saw things differently, trusted him, and told him the truth.**

Exercise #5:

Consider the people you have chosen to surround yourself with. Could you benefit by reaching out to new and different people to gain different perspectives on your challenges and opportunities? Whom could you reach out to in the future with different and maybe even opposing viewpoints? What could you say or do to inspire their trust?

Follow-Up

I think it was Tom Peters who once said, "What gets measured gets done." I think he was right. Here's why.

A few years before the Great Flood of 1993, I attended U.S. Army Airborne School at Fort Benning, Georgia, in what had to be the hottest and most humid month of the year: August.

Georgia in August doesn't have what you would call a comfortable climate. There were days we were so sweaty that our uniforms looked like we had been in the the shower with our clothes on. They were totally soaked.

The airborne instructors were there to teach soldiers how to parachute out of airplanes. They had no desire to play nurse to soldiers who didn't drink enough water and who were likely to end up suffering from heat exhaustion or a stroke.

Every single morning before we went off to training and while we were standing in formation, we were instructed to have a full canteen of water; everyone knew it. One simple instruction was given. That was it. We were grown, motivated, and responsible adults, so what would you expect to happen?

You would expect everyone to show up with a canteen full of water, right? Wrong. There was always one, and sometimes several people, who just didn't do what they were told, for whatever reason.

So every day, while standing in formation, we had our water bottles inspected to make sure they were full. A sergeant would literally come and lift each bottle on each person to make sure that none of them were empty.

You know that old saying "You can lead a horse to water, but you can't make him drink"? Well, if soldiers had water, the sergeants COULD make them drink. And they did.

Every so often, an instructor would stop the training and ask everybody to drink their canteen full of water. Would everyone do it? Follow this simple instruction? No.

That's why the instructors would ask everyone to take the lids off their canteens and hold them upside down over their heads to prove they were

63

empty. Or in some cases, not. Then we would get told to go fill up our canteens, and we would go through the same routine a few more times each day.

While it seemed like they were treating those of us who COULD follow directions like children, it was annoyingly obvious that they HAD to do it. The result was that we—and I'm talking about several hundred people—made it through 3 weeks of physical outdoor training in Georgia, in August, without one single soldier suffering a heat-related injury.

The sergeants who were Airborne instructors knew that they had to inspect what they expected. If only one person became a heat casualty, the instructors still knew that it was unacceptable.

So let's go back to discussing flood duty. I'm in no way implying that my guys needed to be treated like the instructors at Airborne School treated us. However, there were times when things were just really, really hectic and they were being asked to do a lot of different things, and it was reasonable to expect and easy to see how they could simply forget a few instructions.

My platoon sergeant and I both made a habit of double-checking to ensure that our supplies never got too low. We made sure that we called for more dump trucks full of sand—before we needed them. We made sure that we called for more bags—before we needed them. We checked to make sure our vehicles had plenty of fuel,—before they ran out.

Yes, our soldiers were supposed to be doing it too, but the bottom line was that we INSPECTED what we expected and MADE SURE no lapses would cause unnecessary harm. **Inspections and follow-up were critical elements to the success of our operation.**

Avoiding Unnecessary Risks

Our entire unit spent their time in one of two places: either working on the levee or sleeping on a cot in the gymnasium at the high school. My company commander made the decision that alcohol was prohibited completely. And if friends or family members wanted to visit our guys during our shift of downtime, they could come to the gym, but our soldiers had to stay on the high school campus unless they got special permission. And IF they got special permission, they still needed to remain close.

In those two moves, he nipped probably 60% or more of the potential problems at the bud. In fact, in hindsight, looking back on the Sunday morning when we had to call the night shift back out to work on the levee, I realized that had my commander not made, and enforced, those decisions, we might not have been able to round up enough soldiers fast enough to save the north side levee.

I can't even imagine what kind of havoc alcohol could have created, on many different levels, and I, for one, was extremely thankful I did not have to find out. So I gladly give credit to my company commander and his ability to **solve problems BEFORE they occurred!**

High Standards

They say hindsight is 20/20. As I look back on those experiences that summer, I feel compelled to share my thoughts on **the importance of setting high standards.**

I don't take for granted the many blessings I have received, not the least of which is my parents. When I reflect on their advice, in spite of my many attempts to ignore it, it seems that time has proven them to be a lot smarter than I gave them credit for. The old saying that "the older you get, the smarter your parents become" certainly applies to my situation.

One thing they instilled in me from an early age is that when things got tough, I shouldn't pray for them to get easier. Rather, I should pray for additional strength, wisdom, knowledge, and resources that would make me more capable of dealing with whatever challenges I faced.

Almost equally important was their insistence on finishing whatever I started. I was probably six years old when I participated in my first organized sport. I wanted to play, and they said okay, on two conditions: that regardless of what happened,

1.I was expected to do my best, and

2.I was expected to finish what I started.

It didn't occur to me or my brother Carson, upon graduating high school or even college, that these concepts were a big deal. We never even considered if any other options existed, and that kind of thinking was contagious in Ste. Genevieve. Their local high school sports teams have earned numerous state championships, and the banners that hang in their buildings are a testament to the high personal standards that permeate their entire town.

In fact, during the flood it reached almost epic proportions. The volunteers from out of town who didn't have it at first caught it quickly, and help spread it every chance they got. I remember a banner made with a PC dot matrix printer hanging on the wall in the meeting room in City Hall. It said, "We Can Do This."

This wasn't some jolly, feel-good slogan. It was the only option available. This community did their best, and they didn't quit.

Exercise #6:

What personal or professional standards have you set that need to be raised?

Sincere Appreciation

Just shy of 14 days into our mission, we were told that another unit was coming in to relieve us. Our time in Ste. Genevieve was nearing its end. Levees continued to break all up and down the river everywhere, but not our levees—not while we were there, anyway.

I found out weeks later that while the unit replacing us was was there, the levee in the south part of town, mainly protecting farmland along with a few homes and businesses, eventually gave way, but the homes protected by the north and central zone levees continued to hold, and those levees ended up protecting the vast majority of homes until the flood eventually receded.

This community won the battle to get the levees up faster than the river was rising. With the exception of the farmland levee in the south part of town, they kept the levees from giving in, and they won the war too.

Was every home saved? Of course not. But losing a relatively small number of homes, compared with the consequences of having an entire community obliterated, was still tremendous—

and given the circumstances, an ALMOST impossible accomplishment.

The national news media packed up their cameras, lights, and microphones and went away. Why? Because in Ste. Genevieve, it didn't look like there was going to be a disaster to report.

I will never forget the morning we left. It was about 6:30. I could feel the warmth from the sun and the gentle breeze blowing through the trees. It was a beautiful morning, and frankly I don't remember seeing a single cloud in the clear blue sky.

As we stood in formation in the high school parking lot outside of the gymnasium, the mayor came and spoke to our troops. He came to personally thank them for their effort and cooperation in his effort to save his town.

On behalf of the good people of Ste. Genevieve, he gave each of us flowers to bring home to our families. Members of the local high school band were set up in the parking lot, and they played beautifully as our convoy of vehicles rolled out of town.

It really meant a lot to us that they thought enough of us to come and say "thanks" at 6:30 in the morning. The flowers and the band playing just said volumes more about the people and the town that we had gotten to know and love.

As our convoy quietly rolled through the streets of town, to our surprise we saw dads, moms, grandparents, and little children, still wearing their pajamas and rubbing the sleep out of their eyes, standing on their porches, in their front yards, and along the sidewalks. They were waving their hands, waving their American flags, and holding up homemade posters that had little things like "Thanks for saving our town, and God bless you" written with red, white, and blue markers.

What I'm about to share with you I will never forget. I was riding in the front passenger seat of my Humvee, just outside the city limits on our way back to the armory. The driver was talking to me, and as I looked over at him I noticed the sergeant in the seat behind him was crying.

It was Sergeant Elmer Wherely, a much older, but kind and dependable, Vietnam veteran who was also a squad leader in my platoon. I asked him if he was OK.

In a voice not much louder than a whisper, cracking with each syllable that came from his lips, while his eyes filled with tears he was obviously trying hard to hold back, he said, "Lieutenant, when I came home from Vietnam, people yelled at me, spit on me, and said many,

many horrible things. They never said 'thanks.' After all these years, I finally got my parade."

The people in the town of Ste. Genevieve let our soldiers know that they cared and that they genuinely appreciated our effort. Their expression of appreciation was so powerful that when the next unit was activated to take our place in rotation and we got to go home, many of the soldiers in our unit came back on evenings and weekends, and brought their families to come help as civilians, in whatever ways they could as volunteers. They cared too much to let it go. To our soldiers, it had become their town too.

We all have challenges. For me in '93, it was a flood. For you, today, your leadership might be 'needed by your family, by your church, by your children's sports teams, by your company, or by your department at work. My goal in sharing these experiences and the lessons I learned from them is to make those around you glad YOU are the leader when it's YOUR turn to lead!

Exercise #7:

Consider the people who have done and continue to do good things for you. In what ways can you express genuine appreciation and gratitude?

Chapter 7:
Corporate Application of Leadership Principles

Many years have passed since I last put on my Army uniform, but the things I learned about people and how they can work well together still amaze me. It has been my experience since that these experiences and observations apply readily in American corporate environments too. In fact, these principles and strategies might even be EASIER to apply in a corporate setting.

Can you think of a more diverse work environment than the military? In any given military unit, a leader has to work with whatever people they are given. The soldiers are a mixed bag of ages, races, sexes, sexual orientations, and religious preferences, and they come from rural areas, suburbs, and big cities all over the country. The military can be "stuck" with a soldier throughout an entire enlistment period.

By contrast, in corporate America, there is a human resources department and there are employment screening systems in place to help them attract, identify, and retain the best and most talented people. There are management training programs that are supposed to improve productivity. Companies can fire employees who cause problems instantly, and don't have to wait for an enlistment period to end.

Corporations can be as picky as they want. The sky SHOULD be the limit to what THESE teams COULD accomplish with the advantages and flexibility they have when it comes to their personnel selection processes ALONE, assuming they have the training, management, and leadership support in place.

(Special bonus: Additional resources are available at http://www.ReverseRiskConsulting.com that can help your organization hire the right people the first time, and keep them longer.)

When I hear executives at companies large and small talking about their desire to improve employee engagement and empowerment and the discretionary effort of their employees, but see them doing little about it (beyond "token" efforts) because it's "hard, expensive, difficult, complex, etc.," I feel bad for the players (employees) on their team.

I know that there are some (maybe a lot of) players (employees) who feel like they aren't making the cut and/or feel like outsiders. Some don't want to give the company all the contributions they have to offer, and go through each day asking themselves what is the minimum amount of effort required for them to keep their jobs. Some hate their employers and are hostile toward them (both outwardly and in stealth mode), seeking to wreak havoc and cause harm whenever and wherever they can. Others leave to go to work for a competitor or start their own businesses (sometimes taking clients and their most valuable ideas with them), singing "if you can't join them, beat them" as they walk out the door. They want to show their previous employer what they missed out on.

Decisions as Sound as the Facts on Which They're Based

Inclusive leadership is the opposite of exclusionary leadership. It involves and invites different perspectives and human experiences into a decision-making process, rather than paying lip service or downright ignoring them.

I have always believed that decisions are as sound as the facts upon which they are based. It just makes sense, doesn't it?

Think about it. If you're put in a position where you're responsible for making a decision, what helps you make better decisions? The truth and/or an accurate sense of what is really going on.

But how do you know what the truth really is? How do you KNOW what is REALLY happening? Isn't that sense of certainty just your interpretation of the data points you have access to?

If I'm forced to make a decision, I want to see everything I can see. I want to hear everything I can hear. I want to feel everything that I can feel. So do most good leaders.

As long as it is relevant and pertinent, the more I see, hear, and feel for myself, the more confidence I have in that data as the basis for good decisions. I think most people feel the same way to a certain extent.

But are good decisions good enough? Maybe they are, and your ability to make good decisions has led you to a comfortable lifestyle and/or career.

True leaders and visionaries also find ways to see things they can't see. They want to hear things they can't hear. They want to feel things that they can't feel.

They use their own intuition based on what they know, but that's only the beginning. The best leaders actively seek out, question, and evaluate the judgment and wisdom of others. They look at life's challenges not only from their perspective but from those of others as well. My friend Cesar Keller told me that smart people learn from their mistakes, but geniuses learn from other people's mistakes, because it is never as painful, expensive, or time consuming.

Why bang your head against the wall when you can learn vicariously through the mistakes and successes of others? To make good decisions, I believe you have to seek out as much valuable and relevant information as you can about any set of circumstances. And you have to treat the people capable of giving you that information fairly and respectfully so they trust you, want you to succeed, and are willing to help.

Exercise #8:

Who could teach you how they approached a similar challenge to one you are facing? When will you contact them, and what kind of help can you ask them for?

Answers Hiding in Plain Sight

I was reading one of my favorite books of all time, Awaken the Giant Within by Anthony Robbins, and he was discussing the power of our reticular activating system, which is basically our brain's system for deciding what we should pay attention to and what we should ignore. If you think about it, we are exposed to so much stimulus at any given moment that it would be hard to function if we tried to pay attention to everything at once. Even something like sitting on a rocking chair on your front porch could be overwhelming if you had to focus on the temperature, the breeze, the sight and sound of every car that went by, each driver, each passenger, the song on the radio, the sunlight, the shade, every bird, rabbit, or squirrel and what they were doing, every blade of grass, every flower and how each was affected by the wind, etc., ALL AT THE SAME TIME.

In his book he describes an exercise that demonstrates the power of the reticular activating system, and I decided to go through it with a live audience while I was delivering a keynote speech on the topic of diversity for a bunch of managers.

Here's what happened when I gave the following instructions to people in the audience.

I said, "I'm going to give you a memory challenge so you can't write anything down. I'm going to show you a slide containing numerous images, and I want to see how good of a job each of you can do recalling as many red items as possible strictly from memory. All the images will appear on one screen, and you'll only get to look at it for about 5 seconds before I hide the images from your sight."

Then I projected a screen containing 12 separate images, along with the words "How many red items can you recall?" Of the 12 images, there were 9 items that contained red. There was a red rose. There was a red tie on a snowman. There was red on a motorcycle helmet, a wrestling mat, a truck, a Santa suit, a balloon, a ribbon, and some strawberries.

When their 5 seconds was up, I stopped showing the images and threw them a curve ball. It was a total surprise when I asked a question none of them were anticipating. I asked the entire audience to list the BLUE items they could recall instead of the red I asked them all to focus on. They scratched their heads and looked at each other in disbelief as they sat there quietly.

I asked again, "Which images, specifically, contained the color blue? Be certain, don't guess, because I am going to show the images again and everyone will know if you were guessing or accurate."

Then I challenged the entire audience to see if anyone would bet money they could describe more than three items specifically that they knew absolutely, positively, for a fact, contained blue? I got NO takers. Zero. Nada. Zilch.

Then I asked if anyone could positively identify at least two items. Two people, in a large audience of managers, raised their hands. Two people could identify two items with the color blue. Everyone else looked dumbfounded, because they were.

Six images contained blue, and EVERY letter in the sentence "How many red items can you recall?" was written in blue. That means there were 27 letters appearing in the blue font, plus the question mark that was blue, and six of the images contained blue too.

Out of 34 items that contained blue, only two people in an entire audience were able to identify two of them.

Then, in an attempt to provide some contrast, I asked them to raise their hands if they could tell me what red items they could recall. They worked as a group and were able to identify all of the nine red items.

Just as a point of comparison, when I asked how many red items were on that screen, the place erupted. I saw hands flying up from everywhere. I heard confident voices coming out from all over the room, and they weren't guesses.

One person raised their hand and accused me of "tricking" them because I told them to look for the red and then asked them about the blue items. It was time to make my point.

Once again, I showed the images on the screen to everyone, just as I had done before. I showed them the red items and congratulated the group for their team effort and pointed out all the red items they correctly recalled. Then I showed them each blue item they missed, including the letters.

Then I asked the audience, "Did you just not look at everything that was on here? I didn't change it, did I?"

Their eyes hadn't deceived them. They had looked at all the exact same images. They did see what they were looking for in advance, but it didn't mean the things they WEREN'T looking for weren't there also.

Here's the point. The reticular activating system told their brains what to notice and pay attention to.

What am I trying to get through to you? What does this mean to you at home, or at work? Just because you didn't notice something, it doesn't mean that it wasn't there.

How many times have you felt like you knew exactly what happened in a meeting or conversation because you were there and heard everything with your own ears and saw everything with your own eyes? You FELT like you knew EXACTLY what happened. To you, that experience WAS reality. However, based on what you now know about the reticular activating system and how it works both for and against you, are you willing to consider the possibility that you missed some things that might have been important or different from what you perceived at the moment?

Just because you didn't see something, you didn't hear it, or you didn't feel it, it doesn't mean it didn't happen.

Remember that exercise the next time someone comes up to you and presents suggestions or observations that are vastly different from yours. There may be merit to what they are sharing, even if you don't think so at first.

Don't be quick to write off someone else's perspective because it is different from what you thought was reality. In fact, you might be well served to intentionally SEEK people with different perspectives so you have a better base of information on which to base your decisions moving forward.

Exercise #9:

What is a current situation where someone has a different perspective from yours? What part of their perspective might add value to the decision you have to make or the action you need to take? Whom might you need to seek out to get an alternative point of view?

Chapter 8:
Consideration of Alternative Viewpoints

Feeling Awkward...and Different

I grew up in a small town, during a time when diversity wasn't a race or gender concept for me or my friends. The extent of diversity then wasn't even rich or poor. Diversity was based on different classifications and traits. Were you a jock, band member, burnout, or good student?

Things weren't much different in college, except maybe a little LESS diverse, since all of us had to be pretty decent students to get in. The student body is very different now than it was back then. The student body when I attended was primarily white upper-middle-class students, just like me.

I thought I was alright with that. One spring day, I and a couple of guys in my fraternity decided to take advantage of some great weather and took a road trip to Forest Park, just a few miles from downtown St. Louis. We thought it would be fun, so off we went, I and four or five others.

It was an amazing day, and we got some sun, played some Frisbee, and just hung out. Of course, we didn't pack a bunch of stuff or plan much in advance before we took off. Once we got hungry, we decided to go to a local supermarket to get some sodas and some food.

The supermarket we selected was at the corner of Delmar and Kingshighway, in St. Louis City. It was an eye-opening experience I will never forget. You know why? We walked into that place, and whether the other guys said it or not, we all felt the same way. We were the only Caucasians in the whole place. I'm telling you, there was not a customer that looked like us. There was not a manager that looked like us. There was not someone in the meat department that looked like us. There was not anyone in the milk department that looked like us. There was not someone in the produce department that looked like us.

I felt AWFULLY uncomfortable. Every single person was polite to us. Every single person was kind to us. Every single person was professional to us. There was no excuse for me to feel different. The tides were turned. I was the one in the minority. I was the outsider, and all my friends were too. Everyone was different from me, and I felt terribly, terribly uncomfortable. It shouldn't have been a big deal, but it did make us all very uncomfortable.

A few years later, I had a client who was Jewish who wanted to meet with me and my marketing director at a kosher deli to have lunch and talk about business. Everyone was really nice, but we were the only men in the restaurant that weren't wearing the little black hat called a yarmulke. We stood out and felt out of place because of it.

Another time, while I was in California, I was asking for directions to a place called the Winchester House in San Jose, which is a historical sightseeing place my parents brought me to when I was a little kid. I knew I was close, so I stopped in a Burger King to ask for directions. The lady that was working the counter was Hispanic, and I couldn't understand what she was saying to me. I might have been three blocks away, and I spent probably four minutes trying to get directions. I was so frustrated.

I readily admit it. Being different from others makes me feel weird. It's uncomfortable. It is awkward and outside of my comfort zone. But it's not hard to argue that most of life's biggest rewards come to those who are willing to push past what is comfortable.

Exercise #10:

What is one thing that makes you uncomfortable, but you know you should be doing more of it? What small steps can you begin to take?

When the 2016 presidential election took place, I couldn't believe what I was seeing or hearing. To some people Donald Trump was a lying, crooked, greedy scoundrel, and Hillary Clinton was the answer to our nation's prayers because of her experience, among other things. To other people Hillary Clinton was a lying, crooked, greedy scoundrel and Donald Trump was the answer to our nation's prayers because of his experience, among other things.

How could American citizens with access to the SAME information about each of the candidates view both of them so differently? Who was right? Who was wrong? How do you judge?

As a general rule, I make it a point to go out of my way to consider opposing viewpoints, as well as the context in which those viewpoints were formed. On numerous occasions, I've had my eyes opened and my judgement improved because I was at least willing to consider different possibilities beyond those that I could see, hear, or grasp for myself.

If or when you dismiss and/or trivialize the opinions or perspectives of others, your credibility as their leader takes a hit. When others feel like you don't value their thoughts, opinions, or insights, they tend to be much less vested and engaged in contributing their energy and talent toward your endeavors.

It takes discipline and effort. However, I make a habit out of considering opposing viewpoints or perspectives rather than dismissing them. I realize that my perspective based on experience doesn't make me right, or someone else wrong. When I'm in a leadership support role, this habit does make me more valuable to others when they are willing to take my viewpoints into account. And, when I'm the leader and responsible for making decisions, my willingness to consider the value of opposing viewpoints makes OTHERS more valuable to me.

Exercise #11:

The next time you evaluate a "sticky" situation or reflect on one in the past, ask yourself this question: What if the opposite of what I believe about these circumstances were true?

Better or Bitter?

For several years, I had the privilege of working with a man named John Seward. He is African American and old enough to be my father, although he would probably deny it. The only reason I know is that is he's got a daughter my age. He is one of the most savvy businessmen I've ever met, period.

Prior to our working relationship, he was a senior vice president for a company with over 4,000 employees. He answered to the president of this major corporation and traveled all over the world representing his company, and I consider myself very privileged to have had the opportunity to work with him.

I will tell you that any place we ever went together, his dress shoes were polished brighter than mine. His suit was pressed more neatly than mine was. His ties and shirts were wrinkle-free. His car was never dirty, inside or out. If there was a speck of dirt on it, he had it cleaned. His area at the office was impeccable.

I got to work with John closely. He was significantly older and had totally different life experiences from mine. He taught me a lot, and didn't hesitate to open up and share experiences he had with discrimination and prejudice.

He was not bitter about being treated with prejudice, and based on the stories he told me, what he referred to as prejudice was not a matter of opinion or perception—trust me on this. When I asked him questions, he would answer matter-of-factly and describe the time lines and details of his less-than-pleasant interactions.

He could have become bitter and been justified in doing so. However, that was not how he chose to handle his personal life or career. He overcame it by becoming BETTER. He realized that the time and energy that he could invest in complaining about it would pay better dividends if he redirected that time and effort toward his own personal development and training.

We talked about his rise up the corporate ladder. He knew that he needed to be better than his counterparts and had to develop skills, knowledge, and ability beyond those of his peers.

Our personal strength, like our muscular strength, is developed by pushing through resistance. Over the course of his career, he got more resistance in his work environment than many of his peers, and developed greater strength because of it. Regardless of whether or not it was fair and/or voluntary, he developed skills, abilities, and intuition that he wouldn't have otherwise, and was a better executive and human being because of it. I had a sales manager one time that told me, "Mason, you don't get sharp by rubbing up against a feather. When hard times come, take it. Let it mold you. Let it craft you. Let it make you sharper. Let it make you better." John knew this. John lived this. I saw the results.

Exercise #12:

What uncomfortable circumstances, activities, or environments could you embrace in an effort to build personal and professional "muscle"?

Think of the Yourself as the Customer

When it comes to treating customers, employees, or people in general with respect, I have a client in Daytona Beach, Florida, right by the raceway, who shared some insights with me that I'm going to share with you. He invited me to Florida and I toured his facility. I spent two days there and got a ton of great ideas.

His name is Mike Panaggio, and he runs an incredibly successful direct mail company called Direct Mail Express. They have a very simple customer service training program: "**Think of yourself as the customer**." That's it.

When in doubt, think of yourself as the customer. Notice what it doesn't say, and this is a very, very important distinction. It is not think of the customer as yourself. How many times do we do that? Something comes up and you say, "Well, I don't see why they are mad. I wouldn't be." That's because you are looking at the situation from YOUR perspective instead of theirs.

From your perspective, and from your viewpoint, based on your experience, you see the things that only you see. But, if you think of yourself as the customer, from where they are, from their perspective, and consider what they feel from what they experience, you know what? You might change your approach.

Why do they operate that way? Why do they think that way? Why is this so important to them? I think it is because they realize just what I pointed out to you earlier. When most people go to a place and they are the only one "like them" there, they're uncomfortable.

A lot of people will leave and never ever go back to a place they weren't comfortable. So, if you want to encourage people to do business with you, or if you want to foster better cooperation and teamwork with coworkers, it may be worth your time to go out of your way to think of yourself as them. Then create a buying environment or working environment they feel comfortable in.

Who are your customers internally? How about external customers? Does the makeup of the people in your organization or team reflect the makeup of your customer base or your employee base? If not, there is an opportunity to improve your relationships with your customers and your employees by making more them feel more comfortable around you and your team.

I used to go to a small church where the demographic could best be described as the 60 above 60. What I mean by that is that we had about 60 people in the pews on any given Sunday, and they were are all over 60 years old.

When we got a new pastor, he was concerned that the number of people in the pews was too small, and he wanted to build a bigger congregation. So he came up with this plan to have a men's breakfast, where he invited the male members of his congregation into the fellowship hall to talk about how to solve this problem.

When I got the phone call inviting me to the breakfast, I agreed to come.

There wasn't a single person who came that was within 10 years of my age in either direction. I wasn't the youngest, because someone brought a grandson. We were the two youngest, and everyone else was significantly older.

I sat through the meeting grinning ear to ear. Why? Because I was reflecting on my team building experience and couldn't help but be amused by the solutions proposed by the team of people gathered.

When I heard what the more veteran members of our church thought needed to happen to build the congregation, it was the EXACT OPPOSITE of anything that would have appealed to me or people my age.

One suggestion was to have members of the church get together as small groups and go visit other church members at home during the week. If you are retired and lonely and don't have much else to do, then I could see the appeal.

But people like me are in our prime earning years. We work a lot. We travel all the time. When I am with my family, I don't want to be interrupted or have to entertain guests. I want to be with my family.

There were plenty of terrible ideas if their goal was to appeal to anyone under 60. I couldn't take it anymore and raised my hand. Then I told them what I was thinking.

They didn't like it. They looked at me like I was doing something wrong or trying to argue with the pastor. I could see that they didn't want any more of my input, so I kept my mouth shut and tried not to make any more waves. (Does that look, sound, or feel like any meetings where you work?)

A few weeks later, the pastor had a guest speaker. The guest speaker spoke for a while, and it looked like we might get out early that Sunday morning, because surely the pastor wouldn't give a full sermon in addition to a guest speaker.

I was wrong. The pastor delivered his full sermon on top of that, and I was ready to blow my stack.

I had a 3-year-old child and a schedule I kept on Sunday mornings. I went to the gym before church, came home, got cleaned up, and took my son to church. I'd go the service and my son would play in the nursery, usually just with the toys because there weren't any other kids his age there. During that time, my wife got her chance to go the gym and work out. We then would all arrive at home about the same time, have lunch, and start our day together.

Well, that particular Sunday, the service didn't get over until about a half hour later than usual. Once noon passed and it was obvious the pastor was nowhere near finished with his sermon, I started to tune out. All I could think about was how bored and angry my child would be after being stuck in the nursery by himself for that additional time. If I could ever get him to come again, it would be difficult.

Against my wife's advice, I called the pastor and asked for a meeting. That was the final straw, and I felt obligated to present "the truth" of my experience.

As we started our discussion, I told him about a half-day presentation I was hired to deliver to business owners near Milwaukee a few weeks earlier. I explained to him that my presentation was supposed to end at 11:30 in the morning. However, because of lots of audience interaction and lots of additional questions, I did not get to cover all the material I had prepared for the audience.

I explained to him that I always make an effort to deliver more than I promise, and it bothered me that I had more material to share that day than I had time left that morning to deliver it.

I went to the sponsor who hired me to speak and said, "You know, I've got additional material to share. I can finish this exercise and stay as long as you need me to, or I can quit on time, whatever you think is appropriate."

The sponsor offered another suggestion. He thought it might be a better idea to explain the situation to the audience and let them decide if they wanted me to stop on time or wanted me to continue until I was finished. (Another example of making decisions WITH people instead of making decisions FOR them.)

I did exactly as the sponsor suggested. I offered to end the session on time for those who had other commitments or stay longer for those who wanted more.

I asked my pastor what option he thought the audience selected. It didn't surprise me at all when he said he thought that they would all want to stay for the additional information.

He was completely wrong. Not a single person wanted to stay past the time dedicated for the session. Every single person was finished. The evaluations afterward were outstanding, and those attending indicated that they got much more than their money's worth.

We covered more than enough material and they were more than satisfied. I set expectations, and they had other commitments. They had other things at that time that they needed to do, and I would have made a grave error in judgment assuming otherwise.

The sponsor and this experience reminded me in a very subtle way about how important it is to think about situations from my customers' perspective. Moving forward, I wanted my pastor to do the same thing.

When I told him this story, my pastor looked like someone slapped him. He couldn't believe all those business owners in the audience paid money to attend and that they ALL were ready to go at 11:30.

Then I told him how I felt when he went 30 minutes too long the day he brought in the guest speaker. I told him that if that had been my first day in his pews, it would have been my last.

The pastor was a good guy and trying to do the right things for the right reasons, and I felt I owed him the truth and an alternative perspective. He thanked me for pointing it out. I wasn't surprised when he told me that nobody had ever told him anything like that before.

What I am trying to convey to you is a simple point: Whether it is a men's breakfast, a board meeting, a team meeting, or a family meeting, there is tremendous value, wisdom, time savings, and money savings when you involve people with different perspectives in your troubleshooting and problem-solving processes. It's the essence of inclusive leadership.

If you have an obstacle that stands between you and the answer to your problem, try to see it from multiple vantage points. For example, let's pretend the answer to your question is written on the back of a billboard. Getting more people to stand next to you and look at it from the front won't help you. Even if you get people who can see the right side, the left side, the top, or the bottom of the billboard, they still won't see the answer written on the back of it. The objective is to see everything from as many angles, vantage points, and perspectives as possible, either through your own eyes or vicariously through others'.

The interesting thing about solving problems is that you often don't know what you don't know. Sometimes leadership is like trying to put together a puzzle without knowing what the picture is supposed to look like. You just know that there is some solution out there to the problem that you have and you've got to find it. And finding it sooner is better than finding it later.

Sheila has always been one to reach out and relate to people outside of her comfort zone. She told me about a time in college when she was nominated for Homecoming Queen and found favor among diverse groups of people while attending Missouri State University. Because she was an independent, she did not have the backing of any particular fraternity or sorority like many of her rivals did.

Her candidacy rested on the strength of relationships build on trust and kindness, with students living in dormitories and off-campus housing. She reached out and connected with students who, until then, had been overlooked, detached from campus, ignored, and/or taken for granted. She won, and she did so in an unconventional fashion, without the support of the biggest sorority or fraternity on campus.

As the world changes, so must we. Successful leaders and the companies they represent hire and develop people who reflect their marketplaces and business landscapes. They adapt to the changes in their environment.

Exercise #13:

Can you go out and find different people to create teams with a broader range of perspectives, talents, and abilities?

Chapter 9:
Prototypical People and Teamwork

Being from St. Louis, I remember when the Rams football team was known as the "Greatest Show on Turf" and I had season tickets. Our running back, Marshall Faulk, was MVP of the National Football League. He was arguably the best player in the NFL, not just the team.

Marshall was 5'10" tall. He weighed 211 pounds and could run a 40-yard dash in about 4.35 seconds.

What do you think would happen if you put together a team of total Marshall Faulk clones? If every player was an exact replica of the league MVP in terms of size, speed, skill, and experience, it would sound pretty impressive to have that much talent on a team.

But would it be a good team building strategy? I would argue against it. Here's why.

Sure, as a running back, I've seen Marshall throw the ball on a few trick plays, so I know he can throw the ball. But he lacks the height, arm strength, and precision passing ability of an NFL quarterback who has been throwing footballs since he was a little kid.

As a running back, I've seen Marshall catch passes out of the backfield. But again, he lacks the height and vertical leaping ability of the prototypical NFL wide receiver.

I've seen him block for other running backs downfield or try to protect the quarterback on passing plays. But since an average lineman in the NFL is probably around 6'6" and weighs over 300 pounds, Marshall, or teammates built just like him, would be overmatched, overwhelmed, and completely ineffective if they were forced to play the game as linemen. Think about it: a team with 11 clones of the NFL MVP would get slaughtered.

Conversely, consider what DIFFERENT abilities, talents, and perspectives bring to a team. You don't have to say them out loud, but just think about the people you work with and the people you have exposure to. It does not have to be someone that you work with directly. You might have a peer that works in another state or at another level who might have a different perspective than you do, and you might ask them for their input on your challenges or problems. Don't be surprised when they share options you didn't consider. You don't have to be the brainiac. You don't have to be the genius that solves all the problems. You just have to have the ability to go get solutions from other people and then make a decision on which one is best and which one is most appropriate. That's a lot easier, andit's a lot less hassle than trying to figure everything out by yourself.

In my consulting practice (see http://www.ReverseRiskConsulting.com) I work with companies who utilize various skill-, attitude-, and personality-based assessment tools to identify individual strengths and opportunities for improvement. Some of the exact traits and characteristics that are a liability in one context can be an asset in another.

For example, one assessment that we have measures things like sensitivity as well as other important traits related to successful job performance. Consequently, I have had people look at a trait like sensitivity and ask how employees with a LACK of that trait could be an asset to the company.

I have a client that will not hire someone to be responsible for collections if the person is not really low in sensitivity. Why? It's because they know that a highly sensitive person in a role that requires them to become personally involved with or emotionally attached to their clients who are in financial trouble is a bad match. When there is a bad match between what a person brings to the job and the traits required by the job, they often leave quickly (or shortly after they've been trained), or worse, they stick around and perform poorly.

Flexibility is another popular trait that employers like to measure in their job applicants and employees. When would a person with a LACK of flexibility be an asset to an employer or team? Rest assured, there is a place for people who are rigid hard-liners in the workplace. Think about quality control jobs or safety inspectors.

I'm just using a few personality and behavioral traits as examples. There are plenty more. Consider the importance of traits like organization, social need, assertiveness, competitiveness, recognition needs, work ethic, reliability, integrity, and others.

Make an effort to become more aware of the relative strengths and opportunities for improvement in current employees, strategic partners, and future employees while they are still applicants! When you find people with complementary strengths and abilities, you have the "secret sauce" that you'll need to identify, develop, and keep the best people.

Collective Genius

I don't know who he or she is or I would tell you their name, but I've heard of a professional speaker with an interesting approach to demonstrating the power of teamwork, diversity, and inclusive leadership. I heard that this speaker gives a Mensa test or IQ test of some sort to each member in the audience.

Mensa, for anyone who doesn't know, is a society of intelligent people who score in the top 2% on officially recognized intelligence tests. Basically, it is a group of high-IQ people.

As you might imagine, some people in the audience would have an easier time with an IQ test than others. Some may struggle with some types of questions, while others will thrive.

Soon afterward, the speaker suggests an alternative plan. Audience members are invited to work together in small teams and share their knowledge, perspectives, intelligence, and answers.

To nobody's surprise, the results delivered by groups of people working together outperformed those of the brightest individuals who chose to work alone. Better results were also delivered more quickly.

What's the lesson? The lesson is that with a collective unit and team, the work product delivered can, and often does, surpass that of one genius attempting to work on their own. When you combine the life experiences, perspectives, and knowledge of different people, one person can't match it. In a team, there is a power behind "collective genius," and as a leader, it's up to you to make the decisions necessary to tap into it and use it.

Think about the reticular activating system exercise. When the audience worked together, they were able to complete the task they were asked to focus on with perfection. As a team, they were able to identify all the red items. Individually I doubt a single person could have gotten more than six of the nine possible items.

Victim or Victor?

As we learned in our discussion of the reticular activating system exercise, just because you didn't see something, it doesn't mean it wasn't there or didn't exist! Some of you will be a victim of prejudice. Some of you may just think you are, even if you're not.

You have to be honest with yourself. If you lose a sale or get passed up for a promotion and your knee-jerk reaction is to say it was because you're a woman, you have a physical disability, you are too old, your skin is a different color, etc., consider this. Were those the REAL reasons, or are they convenient excuses that are easier to swallow than admitting you weren't as good as you needed to be? Are you SURE that the decision makers who disappointed you didn't see strengths in others that you missed? Are they seeing weakness or liabilities in YOU that you've failed to notice or acknowledge?

I'm not saying there aren't legitimate cases where people are denied promotions or other desirable outcomes for ignorant and discriminatory reasons. It's a shame, but it doesn't go unpunished.

For example, if a hiring manager makes the mistake of choosing a less qualified and capable applicant for ignorant, superficial, and discriminatory reasons, then that manager, the team, and the company will suffer by having to carry the load of a less valuable team member. They will miss out because they are not getting the extra productivity and contributions they would have gotten if they HAD made a better staffing decision.

If a hiring manager CONTINUES to make those same mistakes, given enough time, they can end up with a team of incapable people when they could have a team of all-stars. They suffer. Their team suffers. Their department suffers. Their company suffers, and so do their customers. It's all unnecessary.

Regardless of whether or not you were discriminated against, you have a choice about how to respond to your adversity. You can invest your time and energy in complaining, which may or may not change anything. Or you can apply that same energy to developing new skills, abilities, or better opportunities for yourself.

You could justifiably argue that it's not fair that you have to work harder and become significantly better because you are being discriminated against (which may or may not even be the case). You can invest your time and energy in complaining about it, and that will likely drive others AWAY from you. Don't be surprised if you find yourself working alone and unsupported as a self-proclaimed victim.

Or you can invest your time and energy in getting better and overcoming it, which is more likely to get people flocking toward you and wanting to work with you. When people flock to you and want to work with you, they will help you achieve things that you might not have been able to achieve otherwise. Don't be surprised if you find yourself working as part of a "collective genius" with a team of supportive people as a victor.

Conclusion:
A Challenge to Leaders

If you're a leader, whether in a formal leadership role or not, your success is greatly affected by your ability to make good decisions. Earlier we discussed how decisions are only as sound as the information on which they are based, and how the most helpful information can be attained through leadership, diverse analysis, and multiple perspectives.

I've asked people who felt slighted (because they felt like they were different) to be honest with themselves. I have asked them to consider the possibility, as uncomfortable as it may be to their ego, that they were overlooked or passed over for opportunities because of something else besides their difference. I also suggested that they invest the energy that could easily be wasted in anger, frustration, and complaining toward working harder to develop the skills and abilities necessary to overcome any possible unfair bias.

I am also going to suggest to those of you who are leaders that you've got some extra work to do as well. You need to be honest with yourself. Accept that it may take extra time and effort to include others in your decision-making processes who see things differently than you do.

In the short term, I realize that it takes extra time and energy, and sometimes involves frustration, to understand other people's perspectives when they are different from yours. It takes extra time to search for commonality when it isn't blatant and obviously present to begin with. The extra time time it takes up front is NOT a justifiable excuse for you to exclude all but the yes-men who agree with you and see things the same way you do.

If you're a leader and you don't think it's fair that you should have to invest extra time and effort up front to involve others in your decision making, then realize this. Without investing that extra time and effort, you are working with a self-imposed liability, a pure disability of your own creation that holds you, your team, and your company hostage, and it unnecessarily limits your potential. In the long run, re-work always takes longer and costs more than doing something right the first time.

You can run from discomfort. You can hide from it. You can change jobs. You can change those whom you associate with. You can change your membership at the club. You can do whatever you want. Just because you CAN, it doesn't mean that you SHOULD.

Is that what I am encouraging you to do? No. I am encouraging you to be bold, be yourself, and do what's right, especially if it is uncomfortable. It's harder to do, but it's exactly what can separate you from peers and make you exceptional. It's sometimes helpful to remember that it gets easier as you become more familiar with new people and begin to notice similarities you didn't recognize right away. Focus on the similarities and commonalities as they reveal themselves, and build upon them.

Best wishes!

Appendix:
Exercises in Inclusive
Leadership

Exercise #1:

Evaluate your life experiences and think of at least one thing (lesson, perspective, etc.) that stuck with you. What opportunity did it provide you to learn and develop character, personal strength, and/or awareness?

Exercise #2:

Having a motto, life philosophy, or spiritual theme can be critical. Have you used one in the past? What is a challenge that you are currently facing? What motto have you been using to guide your response to the challenge?

Exercise #3:

Consider some of your previous personal and/or professional obstacles. What opportunities or advantages did they give you? What potential opportunities or advantages can you take away from current obstacles or challenges?

Exercise #4:

Consider the people who depend on you and your abilities. In what ways can you become a better follower?

Exercise #5:

Consider the people you have chosen to surround yourself with. Could you benefit by reaching out to new and different people to gain different perspectives on your challenges and opportunities? Whom could you reach out to in the future with different, and maybe even opposing, viewpoints? What could you say or do to inspire their trust?

Exercise #6:

What personal or professional standards have you set that need to be raised?

Exercise #7:

Consider the people who have done and continue to do good things for you. In what ways can you express genuine appreciation and gratitude?

Exercise #8:

Who could teach you how they approached a similar challenge to one you are facing? When will you contact them, and what kind of help can you ask them for?

Exercise #9:

What is a current situation where someone has a different perspective from yours? What part of their perspective might add value to the decision you have to make or the action you need to take? Whom might you need to seek out to get an alternative point of view?

Exercise #10:

What is one thing that makes you uncomfortable, but you know you should be doing more of it? What small steps can you begin to take?

Exercise #11:

The next time you evaluate a "sticky" situation or reflect on one in the past, ask yourself this question: What if the opposite of what I believe about these circumstances were true?

Exercise #12:

What uncomfortable circumstances, activities, or environments could you embrace in an effort to build personal and professional "muscle"?

Exercise #13:

Can you go out and find different people to create teams with a broader range of perspectives, talents, and abilities?

About the Authors

Mason Duchatschek

Consultant, Author and Keynote Speaker

Mason Duchatschek is an Amazon.com #1 best-selling author, a keynote speaker and a consultant. His ideas have been featured in Selling Power magazine, The New York Times, Entrepreneur magazine, Newsweek, Fox News and numerous other national media outlets.

As the president of AMO - Employer Services, Inc. (http://www.ReverseRiskConsulting.com), he is a business expert and thought leader who knows how to solve common business problems before they occur, particularly those that relate to employee selection, development and retention.

As a volunteer, he served as the president of the Human Resource Management Association of St. Louis. He also served on the Missouri State Council for the Society of Human Resource Management (SHRM).

Mason is also a former U.S. Army officer, official Guinness World Record holder and experienced endurance athlete who has successfully completed multiple Ironman triathlons and a 100-mile ultra-marathon.

To book Mason as a speaker at your next event, visit http://www.MasonDuchatschek.com

Dr. Amy Alfermann

Leadership and Organizational Development Expert

In her roles at Edward Jones, Bunzl Distribution USA, Monsanto and Ameren, Dr. Alfermann gained valuable experience in building organizational development and training functions for companies in many different industries who appreciate their most valuable assets—their people. Currently, she serves as a Manager of Leadership and Organization Effectiveness with the primary responsibilities of leading culture, change, engagement and performance management.

In addition to her role as a practitioner, she stays connected with academia by being an adjunct faculty member at Benedictine University and Colorado Technical University, as well as attending conferences focusing on scholarly research.

She is also an accomplished endurance athlete and an official finisher of multiple Ironman triathlons.

Rev. Sheila Bouie-Sledge

Consultant, Trainer, Inspirational Speaker and Pastor

As the founder, president and CEO of My Diversity Circle (www.revsheilabouiesledge.com) Rev. Sheila Bouie-Sledge teaches and facilitates Living Your Diversity Circle through practical diversity activities for businesses and educational and religious institutions. She plans and develops company programs to enhance employees' lives and strengthen organizations while emphasizing their mission and vision statements.

She has served as a past president of the Human Resource Management Association of St. Louis. At the UMC Annual Conference, she was the chair of the Committee on Religion and Race as well as the Committee on Status and the Role of Women.

Proof

Made in the USA
Charleston, SC
25 November 2016